Fire Fighter (FDNY) Exam

"You never fail until you stop trying" - Albert Einstein

Fire Fighter (FDNY) Exam #1

Test Taking Tips

☐ Take a deep breath and relax

☐ Read directions carefully

☐ Read the questions thoroughly

☐ Make sure you understand what is being asked

☐ Go over all of the choices before you answer

☐ Paraphrase the question

☐ Eliminate the options you know are wrong

☐ Check your work

☐ Think positively and do your best

Table of Contents

TEST DIRECTION

DIRECTIONS

Read the questions carefully and then choose the ONE best answer to each question.

Be sure to allocate your time carefully so you are able to complete the entire test within the testing session. You may go back and review your answers at any time.

You may use any available space in your test booklet for scratch work.

Questions in this booklet are not actual test questions but they are the samples for commonly asked questions.

This test aims to cover all topics which may appear on the actual test. However some topics may not be covered.

Studying this booklet will be preparing you for the actual test. It will not guarantee improving your test score but it will help you pass your exam on the first attempt.

Some useful tips for answering multiple choice questions;

- Start with the questions that you can easily answer.

- Underline the keywords in the question.

- Be sure to read all the choices given.

- Watch for keywords such as NOT, always, only, all, never, completely.

- Do not forget to answer every question.

1

Air mask is generally worn to protect an individual from dust and paint fumes.

Which of the following is the importance of air masks to firefighters?

A) Many buildings store chemicals that become very hazardous when they burn.

B) Recently built buildings contain synthetic materials that release toxic fumes when they burn.

C) Most of the fire-related deaths are due to smoke inhalation instead of burns.

D) All of the above

2

A **fire extinguisher** is a metal cylinder with water or chemicals at high pressure that helps to put out fires.

When inspecting a home or business fire extinguisher, how high on the wall should the unit be placed?

A) Five feet for all units.
B) Less than three feet for any unit.
C) Less than five feet for any unit.
D) Less than five feet for a unit that weighs under 40 pounds, and less than three feet when weighs over 40 pounds.

A **one-family house** has greater privacy than a multi-family house. Advantages include no common doors, walls or linked spaces. It is a free-standing structure in a neighborhood.

Which of the following room will a fire least likely to start in a one family house?

A) Bedroom
B) Living Room
C) Laundry Room
D) Kitchen

An **exit route** should follow the minimum height and width requirements.

Which of the following principles is used to determine the necessary exit width?

A) Constructional structure
B) Width and height
C) Flow and capacity
D) Architectural Design

5

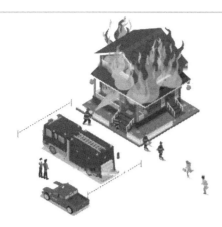

A **structure fire** describes a fire involving the structural components of various types of residential, commercial or industrial buildings.

What is the average response time for a structure fire?

A) 13 minutes

B) 11 minutes

C) 5 minutes

D) 3 minutes

6

By volume, dry air contains 78.09% nitrogen, 0.93% argon, 0.04% carbon dioxide, and small amounts of other gases. Air also contains a variable amount of water vapor, on average around 1% at sea level, and 0.4% over the entire atmosphere.

What is the average concentration of oxygen in the ambient air?

A) 10.95%

B) 20.95%

C) 25.95%

D) 30.95%

Which of the following defines rapid expansion of gases that have premixed prior to the ignition?

A) Endothermic reaction
B) Spontaneous combustion
C) Oxidizer
D) Explosion

A **normal atmosphere** is known to have a 20.8 percent oxygen content. Oxygen deficient atmosphere contains less than 19.5 percent oxygen. On the other hand, an oxygen-enriched atmosphere contains more than 22 percent that presents a significant fire and explosion risk.

In an oxygen-enriched atmosphere, the partial pressure of the oxygen exceeds which of the following?

A) 1.6 Psi
B) 16 Kpa
C) 16 Atm
D) 160 Torr

8

A **heat detector** refers to an alarm that signals the increase in the temperature of a heat sensitive element from the convected thermal energy.

What type of a detector is the heat detector given above?

A) Most accurate
B) Newest
C) Oldest
D) Least accurate

CONTINUE ▶

10

A **fire hose** carries water, foam or other materials in high pressure to extinguish a fire.

Which of the following circumstances is acceptable to stretch a fire hose without taking care not to block a rescue attempt?

A) Salvage operations are underway, and there is no more fire.

B) When the fire hose provides a water stream that facilitates a rescue.

C) It is possible if the fire hose is used to spray nearby structures to keep the fire from spreading.

D) It is never acceptable.

11

A **backdraft** happens when a fire that has consumed all available oxygen explodes when there is more available oxygen typically because of an open window or door.

Which of the following gas ignites during a backdraft from the sudden influx of air into an oxygen-starved room?

A) Carbon dioxide

B) Carbon monoxide

C) Butane

D) Ethylene

12

Classifying fires makes it easier to choose the most appropriate method of extinguishing it. Water is the most commonly used to fight a fire.

For which of the following type of fire would water be most effective?

A) Class A-ordinary combustibles

B) Class B-flammable and combustible liquids

C) Class C-electrical

D) Class D-combustible metals

6

CONTINUE ▶

13

A motor vehicle collision (**MVC**) happens when a vehicle collides with another vehicle, pedestrian, animal, road debris, or other stationary obstruction such as a tree, pole or building.

Which of the following hazards may need to mitigate at an MVC?

A) Fix-a-Flat fluid
B) Vegetable oil
C) Antifreeze spill
D) Kitty-litter

14

Which of the following is the importance of appropriate exit design for everyone to leave the fire-endangered area?

A) Before an untenable atmosphere
B) Without hesitation on the loss of life
C) The shortcut
D) In the shortest possible time

15

Protective equipment refers to a material that helps to protect in certain conditions.

Which of the following is a part of a primary type of protective equipment every fire crew should have on the scene of a fire?

A) A fire hose with an adequate supply of water
B) Proper suits
C) Individual operating air mask
D) All of the above

16

Spontaneous combustion happens by self-heating without an apparent external source of ignition.

Which of the following type of reactions gives rise to spontaneous combustion?

A) Endothermic reaction
B) Exothermic reaction
C) Decomposition reaction
D) Replacement reaction

CONTINUE ▶

Marine firefighting involves fireboats directly applying salty water on structural fires.

What is the most important advantage to having fireboats use salty water?

A) It can extinguish faster than fresh water.
B) It is less corrosive to the contents of the buildings than fresh water.
C) Environmental friendly.
D) It is readily available in the surrounding areas.

18

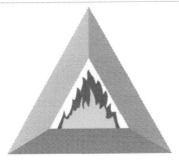

The **fire triangle** is a representation used to aid in the understanding of the three major elements required for ignition.

Which of the following is not one of the elements of the fire triangle?

A) Chemical chain reaction
B) Oxidizer
C) Fuel
D) Heat

Air contains essential substances, such as oxygen and nitrogen. These gases make up about 99 percent of Earth's atmosphere. People need oxygen to live.

Carbon dioxide, a gas that plants depend on, makes up what percent of the air in the sea level?

A) 0.01%
B) 0.02%
C) 0.04%
D) 0.08%

20

Building construction is the stage of adding structure to real property which falls in multiple categories.

Which of the following belongs to Type I construction?

A) Fire resistive

B) Non-combustible or limited combustible

C) Wood frame

D) Heavy timber

21

Egress is described as the right of a person to leave a property. In fire terminology, this term is used for Exit.

Which of the following three separate and distinct parts explains egress?

A) Access to the exit, the exit, and the exit discharge

B) Access to the exit, the exit, and the area outside the building

C) Access to the exit, floor construction, door swing

D) Access to the exit, lighting, signage

22

A **fire extinguisher** is a portable tool that releases water, foam, gas, or other material to put out a fire.

On fire extinguishers, which of the following symbols represents combustible metals or class D fuels?

A) Square

B) Circle

C) Star

D) Triangle

23

Every **hazardous material** is classified to one of nine hazard classes as defined in 49 CFR 172.101 and 173 based on their physical or chemical properties.

Which of the following does not belong to Nine Classes of Hazardous Materials?

A) Flammable

B) Gases

C) Oils

D) Explosive

CONTINUE ▶

24

U.S. fire departments estimated an average of 170,200 home structure fires in 2011-2015 in which 47% were cooking-related cases.

Which of the following covers the majority of cooking-related fires in the United States?

A) Defective stove or oven
B) Ingredients used
C) Types of pots used
D) Unattended cooking

25

If a gas pipe is damaged, a gas leak can occur. Which of the following actions during natural gas leak incident should a fire crew not to execute when responding?

A) Turn electric lights on or off.
B) Trace the source of the leak.
C) Evacuate the building's occupants.
D) Open windows and doors for ventilation.

26

Combustibility measures how quickly a substance will set on fire.

Which of the following is not a factor affecting the combustibility of wood and wood products?

A) Weave type of wood
B) The physical form of wood
C) Content of moisture
D) Thermal inertia

27

Boiling liquid expanding vapor explosion called **BLEVE** is an explosion caused by the rupture of a vessel containing a pressurized fluid that has reached temperatures above its boiling point.

Four conditions must be met to have a BLEVE. Which of the following is not one of them?

A) Liquids have a UEL of 40 PPM or higher.
B) Structural failure of the container
C) A substance cannot be a gas; it must be a liquid.
D) The confined liquid temperature must be above the boiling point at atmospheric pressure when a container fails.

Which of the following describes the lowest temperature a material must be heated for it to ignite and be self-sustaining without an external heat source?

A) Ventilation

B) Accelerant

C) Burnout

D) Piloted-ignition temperature

A **fire** naturally occurs when heat, fuel, and an oxidizing agent (usually oxygen) are present and combined in the right mixture. Fire triangle given above illustrates these three elements a fire needs to ignite.

Which of the following can represent the fire triangle model?

A) Thermal chain

B) Chemical chain reaction

C) Oxidation cycle

D) Fire loop

CONTINUE ▶

Response time is the total accumulated time it takes to respond to a request for service.

How does response time impact flame spread?

A) More than half of confined fires to the floor of origin have a response time of not more than five minutes.

B) Fire is likely to be contained to the room of origin with a response time of not more than five minutes.

C) Half of the fires that extend beyond the building of origin have a response time of six minutes or less.

D) All of the above

A **warning label** is a tag attached to an item, or described in an item's instruction manual, warning the user about its usage risks and may include restrictions that the manufacturer specified.

There are nine hazardous materials warning labels. Which of the following does the class 8 label represent as given above?

A) Poison and poison inhalation hazard

B) Flammable and combustible liquid

C) Explosives

D) Corrosive

Which of the following does the green section of an Emergency Response Guidebook include? (**You can use an ERG – Emergency Response Guidebook to find the answer.**)

A) The table of initial isolation

B) Protective action distances

C) All of the above

D) None of them

33

Common Name: ASPHALT

CAS Number: 8052-42-4

DOT Number: NA _____(Asphalt)

DOT Hazard Class: 3 (Flammable)

According to HAZARDOUS SUBSTANCE FACT SHEET, which of the following is Asphalt's ID number? (**You can use an emergency response guidebook.**)

A) 1000

B) 1888

C) 1999

D) 2017

Storage is vital in handling chemicals for everyone's safety.

Which of the following refers to the most important storage practice for chemicals?

A) Limiting amounts in quantity to avoid expiration.

B) The concentration of flammable solvents should be in specialized metal flammable solvent containers.

C) Containment of liquids should be in unbreakable or double-contained packaging

D) Segregating all incompatible chemicals and store separately.

CONTINUE ▶

Arson is the malicious burning of another's property, or in some cases, the burning of one's property to collect insurance.

Arson is a crime that is the intentional and malicious burning of property. Which of the following is arson?

A) A fire on a patio accidentally started during a grill party.

B) A fire started by an oven in the kitchen.

C) A fire in a table caused by a candle carelessly.

D) A fire set at the front door of a house to bully a neighbor

Natural gas is highly combustible that can produce a massive amount of heat even burning small amounts. Thus, a natural gas leak increases the risk of a fire and explosion since it spreads and goes up in flame quickly.

When firefighters arrived at the place of a natural gas leak, there is no fire yet. What should they initially do after laying a line to handle any possible explosion?

A) Evacuate the occupants of the building.

B) Notify a gas emergency crew.

C) Open windows and doors for ventilation.

D) Start turning off the gas at the curb.

37

Fire crew conducted operations including evacuation procedures at fire-related cases.

Evacuation procedures are designed to remove the personnel from situations in which their lives are in danger.

Which of the following is not a type of Evacuation Procedure?

A) Immediate Withdrawal
B) Sector Withdrawal
C) Tactical Withdrawal
D) Emergency Evacuation

38

Thermal inertia refers to the measure of the velocity of the thermal wave and thermal mass that controls the surface temperature of a material.

What type of burning characteristic does wood with low thermal inertia have?

A) Difficult to ignite
B) Heats up slowly
C) Heats up quickly
D) None of the above

39

The yellow bordered pages of a guidebook are an index list of dangerous goods in numerical order of ID number.

Which of the following is the guidebook referred above?

A) Emergency
B) Emergency Response
C) Firefighter code of ethics
D) Department of Building

40

Mass refers to how much matter is present in an object, on the other hand, **surface area** refers to the measure of the total area the surface of the object occupies.

Which of the following statements about a large mass in relation to its surface area is accurate?

A) More heat energy is needed to ignite the large mass.
B) It is less difficult to ignite large mass.
C) The rate of burning of large mass is the fastest.
D) All the statements above are accurate.

41

Which of the following is a rapid, self-sustaining oxidation process that generates heat and light?

A) Ignition
B) Pyrolysis
C) Vitiation
D) Glowing

42

Moisture content is the measure of a material's water content, and it has an adverse effect on combustibility. Wet wood is more difficult to ignite than dry wood.

Which of the following rise in moisture content would make wood very difficult to ignite?

A) 10%
B) 13%
C) 15%
D) 20%

43

The types of fuel they burn categorize fires. Which of the following is not correct about the fire types?

A) Class A fire involves combustibles such as wood, paper, and other natural materials.
B) Class B fire involves carbohydrates.
C) Class C fire named as an electrical fire.
D) Class D fire involves metals, such as sodium, titanium, magnesium.

44

Which of the following about the spread of fires is not correct?

A) Fire spreads by transferring the heat energy from the flames.
B) Conduction is the passage of heat energy through or within a material.
C) Radiation is the heat traveling via electromagnetic waves with objects or gases carrying it along.
D) Convection is the flow of fluid or gas from hot areas to colder areas.

45

It occurs when ignited fire gases, or incompletely burned fuels, rise to the ceiling and spread out horizontally. Then, smoke appears to start burning suddenly.

Which of the following terms defines the situation explained above?

A) Offensive attack
B) Defensive Attack
C) Mutual aid
D) Rollover

46

Heat energy is the transfer of energy from one thing to another by kinetic energy, usually causing a higher temperature.

What is the approximate heat energy (BTU) of wood per pound?

A) 22,000-25,000
B) 16,000-21,000
C) 10,000-15,000
D) 5,000-9,000

47

Detonation refers to a massive or powerful explosion. Approximately at what speed does a detonation in gases propagate?

A) More than 1800 meters per second but less than 3000 meters per second
B) More than 4,200 meters per second
C) Less than 1400 meters per second
D) Less than 1300 meters per second

48

Total head and **flow** are the main criteria that are used to compare one pump with another. The total head has a relation to the discharge pressure of the pump.

Which of the following defines the total head of a fire pump?

A) PSI (pounds per square inch) rating as the liquid passes through the pipe
B) The static pressure of water at the intake of the pump
C) The energy imparted to the liquid as it passes through the pump
D) The energy imparted to the liquid as it passes through the orifice

49

Which of the following commonly used terms and their definitions about fire is not true?

A) Burnout is a flammable fuel used by some arsonists to increase the intensity of the fire.

B) Backdraft is an explosion that occurs when oxygen is introduced into a room full of hot gases.

C) Dispatch refers to a person or place designated for handling a call for help.

D) An oxidizer is a hazardous material that can combine with adjacent fuel to start a fire.

50

Which of the following definitions about fire terms is not correct?

A) Defensive Attack: An exterior form of attack used when fighting the fire directly or from within a structure.

B) Offensive attack: Method of firefighting in which extinguisher is taken directly to the seat of the fire.

C) Exterior attack: A method of killing a fire by entering the structure.

D) Direct attack: A form of fire attack in which hoses are advanced to the fire inside a structure.

51

A fire-resistance rating refers to the duration for which a passive fire protection system can withstand a standard fire resistance test.

Which of the following is the required fire resistance rating in columns supporting greater than one floor in Type II construction?

A) 0.5 hour

B) 1 hour

C) 1.5 hour

D) 2 hour

52

When a fire exposes to a tank, container shell weakens due to heat and a mechanical explosion occurs.

Which of the following defines this explosion?

A) HAZMAT

B) Dispatch

C) Accelerant

D) BLEVE

SECTION 1 CAREER SPECIFIC KNOWLEDGE

#	Answer	Topic	Subtopic	#	Answer	Topic	Subtopic	#	Answer	Topic	Subtopic	#	Answer	Topic	Subtopic
1	D	TA	S2	14	D	TA	S2	27	A	TA	S1	40	A	TA	S1
2	D	TA	S1	15	A	TA	S2	28	D	TA	S1	41	B	TA	S1
3	C	TA	S1	16	A	TA	S1	29	B	TA	S1	42	C	TA	S1
4	C	TA	S2	17	D	TA	S2	30	D	TA	S1	43	B	TA	S1
5	C	TA	S1	18	B	TA	S1	31	D	TA	S3	44	C	TA	S1
6	B	TA	S1	19	C	TA	S1	32	A	TA	S3	45	D	TA	S1
7	D	TA	S1	20	B	TA	S1	33	C	TA	S3	46	B	TA	S1
8	C	TA	S2	21	B	TA	S2	34	D	TA	S2	47	C	TA	S1
9	D	TA	S2	22	C	TA	S1	35	D	TA	S2	48	C	TA	S2
10	B	TA	S2	23	C	TA	S3	36	D	TA	S2	49	A	TA	S1
11	A	TA	S1	24	D	TA	S1	37	A	TA	S2	50	C	TA	S1
12	A	TA	S2	25	A	TA	S2	38	A	TA	S1	51	B	TA	S1
13	C	TA	S3	26	A	TA	S1	39	B	TA	S3	52	D	TA	S1

Topics & Subtopics

Code	Description	Code	Description
SA1	Fire Science	SA3	Hazardous Materials
SA2	Fire Protection	TA	Career Specific Knowlegde

CONTINUE ▶

TEST DIRECTION

DIRECTIONS

Read the questions carefully and then choose the ONE best answer to each question.

Be sure to allocate your time carefully so you are able to complete the entire test within the testing session. You may go back and review your answers at any time.

You may use any available space in your test booklet for scratch work.

Questions in this booklet are not actual test questions but they are the samples for commonly asked questions.

This test aims to cover all topics which may appear on the actual test. However some topics may not be covered.

Studying this booklet will be preparing you for the actual test. It will not guarantee improving your test score but it will help you pass your exam on the first attempt.

Some useful tips for answering multiple choice questions;

- Start with the questions that you can easily answer.

- Underline the keywords in the question.

- Be sure to read all the choices given.

- Watch for keywords such as NOT, always, only, all, never, completely.

- Do not forget to answer every question.

CONTINUE ▶

1

What is the name of the firefighting tool given above?

A) Drywall hook
B) Pike pole
C) Come-along
D) Rubbish hook

2

Which of the following about the evacuation procedures is not true?

A) Tactical Withdrawal Procedures are for situations in which an offensive (interior attack) is being replaced by a defensive (exterior attack) strategy.
B) Emergency Evacuation Procedures are for situations in which there is a potential structure collapse or hazardous material.
C) Firefighters should take all equipment with them when withdrawing.
D) Sector Withdrawal Procedures are for hazardous situations that require complete withdrawal.

3

There are many factors that can affect fire fatalities in the United States such as education, climate and demographics. However, one key point to consider is the risk of dying across groups of people.

Which of the following is at a high risk of dying in a fire?

A) Men
B) Senior citizens
C) Women
D) Children over five years of age

4

A **vehicle fire** is an undesired conflagration involving a motor vehicle. What percent of fires are vehicle fires?

A) 41 percent
B) 32 percent
C) 22 percent
D) 10 percent

5

Based upon the data of 2017 National Fire Experience Survey, it estimated that public fire departments in the U.S. responded to 1,319,500 fires last year, a decrease of 2% from last year. Of these fires, an estimated 499,000 were structure fires, 5% more than the year before.

Which of the following is the second major cause of residential fires in the United States?

A) Arson
B) Cooking
C) Heating
D) Smoking

6

Flash point is the lowest temperature value at which vapors of the material will ignite when given an ignition source.

What is the flash point for a fluid to classify as combustible?

A) 100 Fahrenheit or more
B) Less than 60 Fahrenheit
C) Less than 90 Fahrenheit
D) Both B & C

7

Residential expresses a relationship with homes, apartments, or any place where people live.

Which of the following percentage of structural fires are residential fires in US?

A) 93 percent
B) 74 percent
C) 50 percent
D) 25 percent

8

What is the correct number designation used by NFPA (National Fire Protection Association) for Fire Officer Professional Qualifications?

A) 1002
B) 1021
C) 1389
D) 1710

9

Pyrolysis refers to the decomposition brought about by high temperatures.

Which of the following would be an accurate statement to describe the term?

A) A decomposition reaction

B) A container failure

C) A physical explosion

D) A rapid, self-sustaining combustion process

10

There are many pieces and parts of ladders used in the fire service.

Which of the following is not a part of the fire service ladder?

A) Ream

B) Rung

C) Rope

D) Pulley

11

A **structure fire** is a fire in a residential or commercial building.

What percentage of all fires in the United States are structural fires?

A) 8 percent

B) 22 percent

C) 29 percent

D) 41 percent

12

An **industrialized country** is a sovereign state that has a developed economy and advanced technological infrastructure relative to other less industrialized nations.

Which of the following statements about fire-related death rates is not true?

A) The United States has the lowest fire-related death rate among all industrialized countries.

B) The United States has the highest fire-related death rate among all industrialized countries.

C) Japan has lower fire-related death rate than the United States.

D) Japan and UK has lower combined fire-related death rate than the United States.

CONTINUE ▶

13

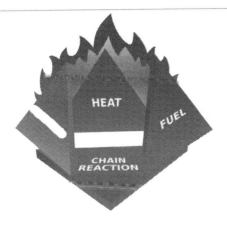

What is the added fourth element in which the fire tetrahedron expands upon the one-dimensional fire triangle?

A) Heat

B) Fuel

C) Oxygen

D) Chemical chain reaction

14

A firefighter feels left out when the other firefighters talk at the station. He thinks that the other firefighters ignore him on purpose and treat him as if he's not part of the team.

What is the best method for him to handle the situation?

A) The firefighter should tell his supervisor that the other firefighters are ignoring him.

B) The firefighter should think Professional and does not bother spending time with them.

C) The firefighter should face with the other firefighters and ask them why they are ignoring him.

D) The firefighter should take an interest in the conversations and spend time getting to know the other firefighters.

A single-family house means that it is a stand-alone structure with its lot intended for one family.

In what room in a single-family house is a fire most likely to start?

A) Livingroom

B) Bedroom

C) Kitchen

D) Bathroom

A firefighter working next to you inside a fire building is injured. He is unsure how badly his hand is hurt.

What would be the best action in this situation?

A) Advise him to perform less laborious duties.

B) Instruct the firefighter to keep his hand motionless and leave the building.

C) Tell the firefighter to continue working.

D) Pull off the gloves to determine the extent of the injury.

CONTINUE ▶

17

If a substance dissolves in a medium, it mixes with the medium and disappear as its original form.

What do you call two materials that do not dissolve each other?

A) Immiscible
B) Miscible
C) Slightly soluble
D) Negligible

18

SIPS is a passive safety system to guard against injury in an automobile.

What does the acronym SIPS stand for?

A) Side impact protection system
B) Supplemental inverted pressure switch
C) Side impact pressure switch
D) Side impact pressure systems

19

NFPA 1710 is a standard that specifies personnel deployment and response times to fires and medical emergencies.

Which of the following is not one of the four main purposes of NFPA 1710?

A) Protect firefighters, ems providers, and the public
B) Decrease amount of time on scene
C) Improve methods of fire prevention, extinguishment and fire control
D) Improve EMS delivery

20

Heat radiation refers to the transmission of internal energy through electromagnetic waves.

In which of the following ways do radiated heat rays travel through space?

A) Sound
B) Light
C) Wind
D) None of the above

21

Solids substances are defined with volume, size, and shape.

Which of the following is not a solid material?

A) Aluminum Foil
B) Cartoon Material
C) Methane
D) Copper

Fire drills are practices of the emergency procedures to be used in case of fire.

Elementary School fire drills are required to conduct 12 times a year. Six fire drills performed during the first three months of the school year.

What is the reason for having half the required fire drills conducted during this time frame?

A) Code of conduct

B) The weather conditions

C) Students in the school can learn fire drill protocols early and often.

D) All of the above

A **natural disaster** results from any catastrophic event that is caused by nature's processes such as flood, tornado, or hurricane.

Which of the following is true?

A) More people die from fires than from all other natural disasters combined.

B) More people die from floods than from all other natural disasters combined.

C) More people die from tornado than from all other natural disasters combined.

D) More people die from earthquake than from all other natural disasters combined.

Which of the following refes to a Type III building construction?

A) Heavy timber

B) Ordinary

C) Non-combustible or limited combustible

D) Fire resistive

25

You are at a local high school doing a fire safety inspection, and a teacher asks if you can help build a bonfire at the baseball game. The teacher tells you she received permission from the fire department and principal as long as a firefighter is on site. You agree to be at the bonfire. After further thought, you discover that the game is on your day off.

Which of the following is the best way to address this situation?

A) Ask a fellow firefighter to attend the bonfire since you are off.

B) Be present at the bonfire considering that your actions will represent your department.

C) Advise the teacher to go ahead without a firefighter and that you have already approved the site.

D) Inform the teacher that you can't attend the bonfire because that is your day off.

26

United States fire departments reported an estimated 1,319,500 fires in 2017. These fires resulted in 3,400 civilian fire fatalities, 14,670 civilian fire injuries and an estimated $23 billion in direct property loss.

Based on the information given above, which of the following is true?

A) Around 3,000 people are injured in fires in the United States each year.

B) Around 15,000 people are injured in fires in the United States each year.

C) Around 15,000 people are injured in fires in the United States each fire case.

D) Around 3,000 people are injured in fires in the United States each firer case.

27

Most of the tools used by fire departments fit into one of the following functional categories such as Rotating (assembly or disassembly), Pushing or Pulling, Prying or Spreading, Striking, Cutting, Multiple Use.

Which of the following type of tool is the tool given above?

A) Brush

B) Striking

C) Power

D) Cutting

28

Which of the following is the right acronym for MVC?

A) Most Valuable Cadet

B) Mass Vehicle Collision

C) Motor Vehicle Collision

D) Master Vehicle Corridor

29

Heat transfer refers to the migration of heat from a high-temperature reservoir to low-temperature reservoir.

Which of the following mechanisms is not a way to transfer heat?

A) Radiation

B) Fusible link

C) Conduction

D) Convection

30

A **knot** is a fastening created by looping a rope or something similar on itself and tightening it.

Which of the following knots is not in the figure eight family of knots?

A) Water knot

B) Fisherman's knot

C) Figure eight

D) Figure eight on a bight

CONTINUE ▶

31

Confined space rescue refers to the technical rescue operations of trapped victims in confined spaces such as underground vaults or storage silos.

Which of the following is the correct meaning for "O" in O-A-T-H commonly used during confined space rescues?

A) Ok

B) Obey

C) Onward

D) Overturn

32

A means of escape is a clear free way to get from any area within a structure to an outside area.

Which of the following statements is not true?

A) Exit doors should open immediately and face outwards into a place of safety outside the building.

B) Sliding doors must not be used for exits specifically intended as fire exits.

C) Each floor plan of a building should have the shortest route to a place of comparative or ultimate safety.

D) Secondary means of escape are mandatory for classrooms but not for bedrooms and living rooms in private houses.

33

Commercial fire is a fire involving the structural components of commercial buildings.

Which of the following is the leading cause of commercial fires?

A) Arson

B) Electrical failure

C) Industrial Accidents

D) Heating

34

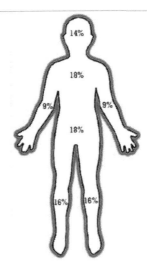

A six-year-old child got severe burns on both of his legs and his right arm during a fire.

According to the figure shown above, what percentage of the child's total surface was burned?

A) 60

B) 41

C) 32

D) 25

CONTINUE ▶

35

An **egress window** is a large enough window for entry or exit in case of an emergency.

According to the code, what is the minimum required size of a new egress window?

A) 6.0 sq ft

B) 5.7 sq ft

C) 5.5 sq ft

D) 5.0 sq ft

36

Extrication means to release from an entanglement or difficulty. What type of extrication tool is given above?

A) Power ram

B) Air chisels

C) Highline pistol

D) Hydraulic ram

37

Outdoor fires are the sweeping and destructive conflagration especially in a wilderness or a rural area.

Based on the average estimate of fires annually, what percent of fires are outdoor fires?

A) 41 percent

B) 29 percent

C) 8 percent

D) 2 percent

38

In a fire, 40% of the building burns. If the building is 600 square feet, how many square feet has not been affected by the fire?

A) 560

B) 360

C) 240

D) 40

CONTINUE ▶

39

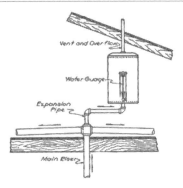

Gravity water tanks refer to the water storage tank that stored water at atmospheric pressure and distributed by gravity flow in a downfeed system.

Which of the following is not a method for heating gravity tank water?

A) Steam coils inside tanks

B) Solar heating of elevated steel tanks

C) Injecting warm air

D) Gravity circulation of hot water

40

Knowing the purpose of using firefighting equipments can secure that they could be of help. Some firefighting equipments are given below.

Which of the following is not a correct explanation about the usage of the firefighting equipment?

A) Gasoline Circular Saw is a gasoline engine equipped with blades which are used to cut masonry, steel, etc.

B) A stretcher is a portable cut on wheels used to transport injured or ill victims.

C) Gasoline Hydraulic Hurst Tool is a tool powered by a hydraulic gasoline engine used to draw water from pools, ponds, etc.

D) The backboard is a sturdy piece of board used to prevent injured victims from moving before they are transported.

A **pressure tank** is a tank in which a liquid or gas stored under pressure higher than atmospheric.

Which of the following is the limitation to take note when using pressure tanks in automatic sprinkler protection?

A) The lack of water stored
B) The lack of pipe size
C) The lack of knowledge of fire department personnel
D) The outside power sources can affect the operation.

Firefighter Rivera finished the fire academy at the head of her class. She acted arrogantly about her accomplishments. After receiving her station assignment, she put minimal effort into station and district drills. Firefighter Rivera was known as a stuck up person. This perception prompted her teammates to treat her as an outsider.

How should Firefighter Rivera handle this situation?

A) Firefighter Rivera should continue with her work and ignore the issue.
B) Firefighter Rivera should engage more with the other firefighters.
C) Firefighter Rivera should apologize for her actions and make an effort to improve her relationship with teammates.
D) Firefighter Rivera should notify her manager that the other firefighters are against her.

43

Low-pressure hydrants can be classified in different categories. "double" hydrants can supply two engines; "single" hydrants can only supply one engine; and "suction" hydrants come from a static source.

Based on this paragraph, which of the following is true?

A) A "double" hydrant is from a static source.

B) A "single" hydrant can only supply one engine.

C) A "suction" hydrant can supply two engines.

D) A "single" hydrant is a high-pressure hydrant.

44

Which of the following describes the process of removing hot smoke and gases from inside of a building by force or convection through an improvised or existing opening?

A) Rollover

B) Flashover

C) Backdraft

D) Ventilation

45

Fire Department Report					
Company	Number of Trucks	Total Number of Calls Received	Total Number of Calls Dispatched	Number of Fire Calls Worked	Number of False Alarms
A	3	101	90	60	12
B	2	99	85	58	7
C	5	412	274	198	22
D	4	110	72	56	13
E	7	623	428	212	109
F	6	519	275	168	33
G	4	228	102	69	18

Which of the following is the average number of trucks for companies that dispatched more than 100 calls?

A) 6.2

B) 5.4

C) 5.2

D) 4.8

Ladder length	# of people to carry the ladder
10	2
20	3
30	4
40	5

Ladder size and the number of people needed to carry the ladder is in the above table.

Which of the following shows the correlation between the length of a ladder and the number of firefighters needed to carry that ladder?

A) There is a linear relationship between the length of the ladder and the number of people needed to carry it.

B) The longer the ladder, the fewer the number of people needed to carry it.

C) As the ladder length triples, the number of people needed to carry it doubles.

D) As the ladder length doubles, the number of people needed to carry it also doubles.

Length of a ladder is 60 meters. It is 36 meters away from the base of the building. What is the height that the ladder reaches?

A) 60

B) 52

C) 48

D) 36

48

Which of the following about fire-related terms is not correct?

A) Majority of fire-related deaths in the United States are a result of careless smoking.

B) FEMA is The United States Fire Administration which is managed by the Department of Homeland Security.

C) NFPA called The National Fire Protection Association, a research group which sets many standards and best practices for firefighting, equipment, and fire protection in the United States

D) The leading cause of home fires in the United States is cooking.

49

The water tank of a fire truck is 4-meter length, 3 meters wide and 2 meters high. If water is pumped at speed if 2-meter cube per minute, how many minutes will it take to finish the water in the tank?

A) 96

B) 48

C) 24

D) 12

50

Some firefighter terms and their meanings are given below. Which of the following is not a correct explanation?

A) MVA: Motor Vehicle Accident

B) Bus: Usually refers to a firefighter truck

C) Mutual aid: An agreement between nearby fire companies to assist each other during emergencies

D) Decay: The fire consumes available fuel, temperatures decrease, the fire gets less intense.

51

Which of the following fire terms is not defined correctly?

A) Flashover is the sudden, simultaneous ignition of everything in a room.

B) Fire flow is the amount of water being pumped onto a fire.

C) Backdraft is a fire phenomenon caused when heavy smoke is removed from a room.

D) Rollover occurs when ignited fire gases spread out horizontally.

For safety, firefighter wants to place the base of the ladder at a distance equal to 20% of its length away from the base of a building.

If the ladder is 60 feet tall, how far away from the base of the building should he place the ladder?

A) 24 feet

B) 20 feet

C) 12 feet

D) 10 feet

SECTION 2 GENERAL KNOWLEDGE

#	Answer	Topic	Subtopic	#	Answer	Topic	Subtopic	#	Answer	Topic	Subtopic	#	Answer	Topic	Subtopic
1	B	TB	S1	14	D	TB	S3	27	B	TB	S1	40	C	TB	S1
2	C	TB	S1	15	C	TB	S1	28	C	TB	S1	41	A	TB	S1
3	B	TB	S1	16	B	TB	S3	29	B	TB	S1	42	C	TB	S3
4	C	TB	S1	17	A	TB	S1	30	A	TB	S1	43	B	TB	S1
5	C	TB	S1	18	A	TB	S1	31	A	TB	S1	44	D	TB	S1
6	A	TB	S1	19	B	TB	S1	32	D	TB	S1	45	C	TB	S2
7	B	TB	S1	20	B	TB	S1	33	A	TB	S1	46	C	TB	S2
8	B	TB	S1	21	C	TB	S1	34	B	TB	S2	47	C	TB	S2
9	C	TB	S1	22	D	TB	S3	35	B	TB	S1	48	B	TB	S1
10	A	TB	S1	23	B	TB	S1	36	B	TB	S1	49	D	TB	S2
11	C	TB	S1	24	A	TB	S1	37	A	TB	S1	50	B	TB	S1
12	A	TB	S1	25	B	TB	S3	38	B	TB	S2	51	C	TB	S1
13	C	TB	S1	26	B	TB	S1	39	A	TB	S1	52	C	TB	S2

Topics & Subtopics

Code	Description	Code	Description
SB1	Basic Concepts	SB3	Human Relations
SB2	Mathematical Skills	TB	General Knowledge

TEST DIRECTION

Read the questions carefully and then choose the ONE best answer to each question.

Be sure to allocate your time carefully so you are able to complete the entire test within the testing session. You may go back and review your answers at any time.

You may use any available space in your test booklet for scratch work.

Questions in this booklet are not actual test questions but they are the samples for commonly asked questions.

This test aims to cover all topics which may appear on the actual test. However some topics may not be covered.

Studying this booklet will be preparing you for the actual test. It will not guarantee improving your test score but it will help you pass your exam on the first attempt.

Some useful tips for answering multiple choice questions;

- Start with the questions that you can easily answer.

- Underline the keywords in the question.

- Be sure to read all the choices given.

- Watch for keywords such as NOT, always, only, all, never, completely.

- Do not forget to answer every question.

1

Which of the following is used for making holes in metal by a firefighter?

A) Auger drilling device

B) Masonry drill bit

C) Carbide drill bit

D) Dato set

2

A fire crew passed by and instructed you to help the spread of fire in the multi-room building.

Which of the following should you initially do?

A) Close the doors between rooms or suites.

B) Soak down the adjoining rooms or suites.

C) Open all of the windows.

D) All of the above

CONTINUE ▶

Two firefighters are doing a fire inspection on a daycare building when the operator tells them, "This facility got inspected before, and everything is safe. Why don't you gentlemen get going and complete your other inspections?"

What is the probable reason for the owner's behavior?

A) He is sure that the building is safe because he stated that inspection was done before.

B) The operator is looking for some favor from the department.

C) There are code violations that he does not want to get discovered.

D) Operator values the department and does not want to waste the fire fighter's time.

When a firefighter arrives at the scene of the fire, a neighbor is trying to give him some information.

Asking which of the following questions would be the most important for the firefighter?

A) Do you know if anyone is inside?

B) Did you see anyone leave the building?

C) Who lives at this address?

D) Do you know when and how the fire started?

5

Which of the following is not a factor when assessing a fire emergency?

A) If the fires were violated
B) Type of building material
C) The wind's direction
D) Occupants of building

6

While inspecting a strip mall during fire prevention activities, a firefighter observes a severe fire violation inside a store. The store owner is a relative of the firefighter.

What should the firefighter do in this situation?

A) Issue a stricter penalty than required to avoid suspicious in favoritism.
B) Inform the owner of the violation and issue the appropriate penalty.
C) Leave the store immediately to avoid family conflict.
D) Inform the owner of the violation but take no action.

7

Which of the following Fahrenheit values is equivalent to -10°C?

A) 22°F

B) 32°F

C) 14°F

D) 18°F

8

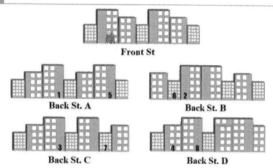

Front St

Back St. A

Back St. B

Back St. C

Back St. D

Size up is the process of gathering and analyzing information that will influence decisions fire officers make and actions firefighters take.

You are conducting a size up on a building, and are doing a walk around. While looking at the front of the building(s) on the top, which of the following would you expect the rear of the building(s) to look like?

A) Back St.A

B) Back St.B

C) Back St.C

D) Back St.D

9

Which of the following tools is used to cut locks, barb wire fence, and steel bars?

A) Bolt cropper

B) Halligan bar

C) Tinner snips

D) Kelly tool

10

Two tourists visiting the country are outside your quarters and ask you if they can take a picture of themselves sliding down the firehouse pole.

What would be the best response?

A) Explain to the tourists that you don't have the authority to allow them to slide the pole.

B) Allow both to slide down the pole and take pictures.

C) Tell them this type of action is unacceptable in the United States.

D) Allow one visitor to slide the pole and the other to the take picture.

CONTINUE ▶

According to **Firefighting Procedures**, firefighters must psychologically adjust to a "no rush" approach during Vacant Building Fires. In these buildings, the life hazard is only to the firefighter. A slower, more cautious operation is indicated.

According to the explanation given above, why do firefighters take a "no rush" approach when operating fires in vacant buildings?

A) Electricity and Gas Utilities are usually already shut down inside the building.

B) The life hazard is generally minimal.

C) Depending on the various weather situations their mobility will be limited.

D) Vacant building's Property Values are less than others.

Explosion refers to a violent outburst of something such as caused by bombs. You reached the area where an explosion occurred.

Which of the following can prove that the explosion was an accident?

A) The structure shows signs of implosion effects.

B) Walls of the building were blown outward at their base.

C) The explosion shattered a lot of objects.

D) A crater area shows significant damage.

During large firefighting operations in Fulton County, fire companies in neighboring Hamilton County temporarily relocated to the firehouses in Fulton County.

What is the primary reason behind this?

A) Allow Hamilton County firefighters to become familiar with the Fulton County structures and hydrants.

B) Provide backup fire coverage for Fulton County.

C) Provide security for the firehouses in Fulton County.

D) So the Hamilton County fire chiefs can critique on Fulton County firefighting tactics.

Firefighters arrive on the scene of an accident. Which of the following is the first thing they should do?

A) Promptly check the victims for injuries.

B) Redirect traffic until the police arrive.

C) Stop the flow of traffic to the area.

D) Call for police and ambulatory assistance.

15

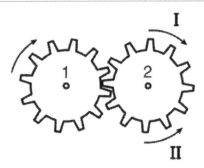

If a force is applied to Gear 1 in the shown direction, which of the following will be true if the radius of Gear 1 and Gear 2 are different?

A) Gear 2 will be rotating clockwise in direction I

B) Gear 1 and Gear 2 will be rotating in opposite directions.

C) Number of rotations of both gears will be same.

D) The gear with the bigger radius will rotate more than the other gear.

16

The tool shown above is for forcible entry by firefighters. What is the name of this tool?

A) Maul

B) Halligan tool

C) Kelly tool

D) Pry bar

17

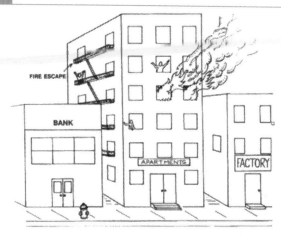

In the figure above, a fire in an apartment is shown. Which of the following is NOT true? **(The ground floor is the first floor.)**

A) A firefighter can cross directly to the roof of the building on fire from the factory.

B) There is a person on a fire escape on the fourth floor.

C) The hydrant is in front of the bank.

D) The fire is on the fourth floor.

18

A firefighter was inspecting an automobile repair garage. He observed several dangerous conditions.

Which of the following is the most critical situation in terms of fire hazard?

A) Way to the exit door in the garage is not passable.

B) A mechanic is working next to a gas tank while he is smoking.

C) An electric heater is heating the garage.

D) There is no fire extinguishing equipment in the garage.

19

Cutter could be handy in a situation where a ceiling has collapsed, and a firefighter becomes entrapped.

Which of the following is the name of the cutter given above?

A) Hole cutter

B) Wire cutter

C) Keyhole cutter

D) Box cutter

CONTINUE ▶

20

Tools are necessary to carry out operations and objectives.

What is the common tool found on many firefighters across the country?

A) Circular saw

B) Concrete saw

C) Carbide chain

D) Chainsaw

21

Suppose there is a fire in the subway. When evacuating passengers through the subway tunnel, which of the following firefighters must do first?

A) Start evacuating the passengers immediately.

B) Locate the emergency exit in the tunnel.

C) Call the train master for assistance.

D) Remove electrical power from the rail.

22

Firefighters show good manners and character such as honesty, professionalism, and integrity.

A firefighter driving to home at the end of his shift, notices a burglar alarm system ringing in a local business. What action should the firefighter take in this situation?

A) Don't get involved he is already done with his shift.

B) Notify the police via the nearest public phone or his cell phone.

C) Assume the owner is inside opening the store for the day.

D) Continue to his house and inform his fellow firefighters of the matter.

23

Firefighter John sustained a severe injury while operating at a fire. Upon returning to the firehouse, Firefighter Jack received a call from John's wife, asking to speak to John. Jack informed her that John was at the hospital because he got injured while fighting a fire.

Which of the following defines Jack's action?

A) Improper; She had to tell her to come to the firehouse.

B) Improper; Jack has not the authority to make such a notification.

C) Proper; Families should know if there is a severe injury.

D) Proper; he has to inform John's wife.

There are different types of **saws** that firefighters use. A circular saw is a power-saw that cuts various materials using a rotary motion spinning around an arbor. It is a tool for cutting materials such as wood, plastic, or metal and may be hand-held or mounted to a machine.

Which of the following types of saws is not an electrically powered saw?

A) Chainsaw

B) Bandsaw

C) Hacksaw

D) Jigsaw

During an uncontrolled fire, firefighters have followed proper procedures and have just found that the fire has extended into the wall.

Which of the following is the next way that the firefighters should do?

A) Put out the fire in the wall.

B) Put out the fire in the fireplace.

C) Tear open the wall with axes.

D) Check if the necessary equipment is ready for use.

There is an uncontrolled fire, but the fire has not spread to the inside of the room. There is also a canvas cover in front of the fireplace.

Which of the following is the next step the firefighters should do?

A) Put out the fire in the fireplace.

B) Put out the fire in the walls and floor.

C) Tear open the walls and ceiling with axes.

D) Check if the fire has extended into the floor.

CONTINUE ▶

27

In a fire, the whole building is in flames. As soon as the fire is under control which of the following search is necessary to conduct?

A) No search because whole building is in flames.
B) A primary search followed by a secondary search.
C) A primary search.
D) A secondary search.

28

Which of the following best describes siphoning?

A) Bonding two pieces of plastic
B) Transferring liquid through a tube
C) To lift a heavy object.
D) Joining two pieces of metal

29

Kurt and Paul pulled off a 100' section of wildland hose and a nozzle to fight the grass fire.

What is the type of nozzle used in the picture given above?

A) Dual
B) Duo
C) Forester
D) Master

30

A **self-contained breathing apparatus** (SCBA) is a device worn by rescue workers such as firefighters to provide air in an immediately dangerous atmosphere.

Firefighter Alpha says there are two types of self-contained breathing apparatus used by the fire service. They are open circuit and closed circuit. Firefighter Beta agrees with Alpha and states that closed circuits are used more frequently than an open circuits.

Based on the information given above, which of the firefighters is correct?

A) Both Firefighters
B) Firefighter Alpha
C) Firefighter Beta
D) Neither Firefighter

31

The fire has not extended to the inside of the room, so the firefighters put a canvas cover in front of the fireplace.

What is the next thing the firefighters should do at the scene of this open fireplace?

A) Put out the fire in the fireplace.
B) Put out the fire in the ceilings, floors, and walls.
C) Tear open the ceilings, floors, and walls.
D) Determine if the fire has reached the ceilings, floors, and walls.

32

A firefighter-operating vehicle is hit from behind by a taxi vehicle. The firefighter got no injuries in the accident.

What is the first action the firefighter should take during this event?

A) Call 911.
B) Make sure nobody in the other vehicle is injured.
C) Counsel the taxi driver but take no summary action.
D) Issue a summons.

33

Firefighter Johnson is searching underneath beds and inside closets of a burning home. What is he looking for?

A) Children: Often they use these places to hide from a fire.
B) Entry points from outside:Closets on exterior walls can be an easy way for entry from outside.
C) Electrical panels: Panels can be in closets.
D) Smoldering items: These places most often contain those items.

CONTINUE ▶

Firefighters often are required to remove trapped people in elevators. There is a fire in the building, and someone in the elevator is injured. A firefighter is attempting to free the injured man, but he determines that all the hallway doors leading into the elevator shaft are not passable.

Which of the following should the firefighter do?

A) Try to remove the trapped person.
B) Wait for help from other firefighters.
C) Call for an elevator mechanic.
D) Call for an ambulance.

Firefighter Zaire is preparing a report about a recent explosion. He will include the following statements in the report.

K. I quickly treated the pedestrian for the injury.

L. The explosion caused one of the glass windows in the building to shatter.

M. After the pedestrian got treated, Police Department was called to ask for help in evacuating the area.

N. After the explosion I saw a pedestrian who was bleeding from the arm.

In which of the following orders firefighter Zaire should arrange the statements in his report?

A) L, M, K, N
B) K, L, N, M
C) L, N, M, K
D) L, N, K, M

Firefighters need portable ladders to rescue people.

Which of the following is the greater threat to the firefighters' safety while positioning a portable metal ladder for a rescue?

A) A person who is standing next to an open window is waiting to be rescued.

B) A person who is in a long robe is waiting to be rescued.

C) Electrical wires that are close to the metal ladders used by the Fire Department.

D) Tree branches that are very close to the ladder.

After driving to a wildfire, firefighter Ted drives into a grassy area, stops, parks the truck and continues to put out a 60 X 60 grass fire. The winds are coming out of the west at 18 mph.

What is wrong with this scenario?

A) He is still parked in the green although it is a land fire.

B) He should not have put the truck in the park in case he needs to get out of there fast.

C) The high winds are a red flag warning.

D) Nothing, the firefighter, is doing everything correctly.

Investigators assumed the suspects for the three fires that took place within a three-week period were those who were running from the building on fire. Each arsonist's description is as follows.

• Fire #1. (April 8)- male, white, teenager, 5'5", 175 Ibs., cap, tattoo on upper left arm, short-sleeve gray shirt, black pants, and black shoes.

• Fire #2. (April 14) - male, white, teenager, 5'5", 145 Ibs., white cowboy hat, large scar directly over the eyebrow, short sleeve shirt, blue pants, and black shoes.

• Fire #3. (April 22) - male, white, teenager, 5'5", 140 Ibs., short brown hair, large- sized sunglasses, short sleeve blue shirt, blue jeans, and black sneakers.

On September 24, a fourth fire occurs near the Bay Housing Project and a suspect spotted once again. Suspect's description is as follows.

• Fire #4. (April 24) - Male, white, teenager, 5'5", 143 Ibs., short brown hair, large scar directly over the eyebrow, short sleeve gray shirt, black pants, and black shoes.

With the given description of the suspects for the first three fires, should the suspect for Fire #4 also be part of the other fire number cases?

A) 1 and 2, but not 3

B) 2 and 3, but not 1

C) 2, but not 1 or 3

D) 2 and 3

Scanning a burning building is one of the most vital and dangerous aspects of a firefighter's job. Searches are divided into two main types which are the primary and secondary. These searches are different and they require different tactics.

Which of the following is the difference between a primary and secondary search?

A) A primary search is mandatory.

B) A secondary search is mandatory.

C) In a secondary search, time is the most critical factor.

D) In a primary search, time is the most critical factor.

How many gears are turning clockwise in the
illustration given above?

A) 6

B) 5

C) 4

D) 3

55

SECTION 3 BASIC SKILLS

#	Answer	Topic	Subtopic	#	Answer	Topic	Subtopic	#	Answer	Topic	Subtopic	#	Answer	Topic	Subtopic
1	C	TC	S3	11	B	TC	S1	21	D	TC	S2	31	A	TC	S1
2	A	TC	S1	12	B	TC	S1	22	B	TC	S1	32	A	TC	S1
3	C	TC	S2	13	B	TC	S1	23	B	TC	S2	33	A	TC	S2
4	A	TC	S1	14	A	TC	S2	24	C	TC	S3	34	C	TC	S2
5	A	TC	S2	15	B	TC	S3	25	D	TC	S1	35	A	TC	S2
6	B	TC	S2	16	B	TC	S3	26	A	TC	S1	36	C	TC	S1
7	C	TC	S1	17	A	TC	S1	27	D	TC	S2	37	A	TC	S2
8	A	TC	S2	18	B	TC	S1	28	B	TC	S3	38	B	TC	S2
9	A	TC	S3	19	B	TC	S3	29	C	TC	S3	39	D	TC	S2
10	A	TC	S1	20	D	TC	S3	30	B	TC	S1	40	D	TC	S3

Topics & Subtopics

Code	Description	Code	Description
SC1	Situational Awareness	SC3	Mechanical Aptitude
SC2	Judgement & Reasoning	TC	Basic Skills

Made in the USA
Middletown, DE
11 February 2024

49527158R00035